A TASTE OF MARVEL

SNACKS

A TASTE OF MARVEL

SNACKS

Bite-Size Recipes in a Snack-Size Book

INSIGHT EDITIONS

SAN RAFAEL · LOS ANGELES · LONDON

CONTENTS

7	Introduction
9	Sweet and Salty Peanuts
13	Seasonal Market Veggies and Hummus
17	Biergarten Soft Pretzels and Spicy Honey Mustard
21	Ceviche Tigers Milk
25	Arañitas
29	Kraving Veggie Dumplings
35	Cheese Arepas
39	Pierogis
45	Cheese Knishes
49	Cassava Fries
53	Charred Okuru
57	Plantain Chips

61 Okra Fritters
64 Harissa-Spiced Popcorn
66 Boiled Mtedza
68 Zouma Bowa
71 Vegetable Samosas
75 Shrimp Ceviche
79 Negasonic Warheads
83 Chick-Arrones
86 I'm a Real Fungi
89 Street-Corner Street Corn
92 Pool-Tine
96 Fireballs
100 Bulging Mussels
105 Pete's Meat Pies

DIETARY KEY

V: Vegetarian
V*: Easily Made Vegetarian
V+: Vegan
V+*: Easily Made Vegan
GF: Gluten Free
GF*: Easily Made Gluten Free

INTRODUCTION

Welcome to *A Taste of Marvel: Snacks*, a selection of tasty recipes inspired by Marvel super heroes, Spider-Man, Black Panther, and Deadpool. From Seasonal Market Veggies and Hummus, Cheese Knishes, and Plantain Chips to Pool-Tine and Pete's Meat Pies, this snack-size cookbook includes a variety of recipes, including vegetarian, vegan, and gluten-free options, to prepare snacks for yourself, family, and friends while sharing your love of Marvel characters and stories. Enjoy!

SWEET AND SALTY PEANUTS

Ah, the circus. Just the mention of it brings up memories from when I was a wee Spider-Lad seeing everything from the trapeze artists to the clowns for the very first time. I even got to feed the elephants. The smell of beer nuts takes me back to that. Though I try to block out a memory from a few years later, when I went back as an adult and had to tangle with the Circus of Crime for the first time. Let's just say they don't give me the same nostalgia feels. Though I will admit that fighting them center ring at Madison Square Garden did scratch my itch to ham it up in front of a capacity crowd. (I want to make a Spider-Ham joke so bad here, but he's a multiversal treasure who deserves better than that. I really should be applauded for my restraint.) I suppose you can also chalk up some lapses in memory to the fact that their leader, the Ringmaster (so on the nose with that one), hypnotized me and sent me after Daredevil. Only some clever sleight of hand from old Horn Head and, oddly enough, the smell of beer nuts snapped me out of my stupor. I made sure to grab a bag, and the recipe, before I left MSG. Got to feed the elephants again, too.

—Spider-Man

SWEET AND SALTY PEANUTS

Prep Time: 30 to 45 minutes
V, V+*, GF | **Yield:** 2 servings

½ cup water
1½ cups granulated sugar
4 cups unsalted and unroasted peanuts
1 tablespoon kosher salt
4 tablespoons granulated honey (omit if vegan)
1 teaspoon vanilla paste
½ teaspoon ground cinnamon

1. In a large nonstick sauté pan, bring water and sugar to a simmer on medium-high heat.
2. Add peanuts and salt. With a wooden spoon, keep stirring and cooking continuously on medium heat.
3. After about 8 to 10 minutes, as sugar begins to crystallize, add honey, vanilla paste, and cinnamon powder. Remove from heat and pour onto greased parchment to cool a bit before serving.
4. Serve warm and enjoy.

SEASONAL MARKET VEGGIES AND HUMMUS

I'm not without my own cooking skills, you know. When called upon I can put together a mean plate of crudités, especially when I'm invited to a picnic out here at Silver Lake Park, or Willowbrook Park, or Clove Lakes Park (geez, no wonder they call Staten Island "the borough of parks"). Take note of my culinary genius, I'm not sharing a lot of these. Appreciate this special glimpse into Spidey's kitchen. You can thank me later.

—Spider-Man

SEASONAL MARKET VEGGIES AND HUMMUS

Prep Time: 45 minutes
V, V+, GF | **Yield:** 6 to 8 servings

1 small clove garlic, minced
4 tablespoons tahini
⅓ cup extra-virgin olive oil, plus 1 tablespoon for plating, divided
4 tablespoons fresh lemon juice
One 15-ounce can chickpeas, drained and rinsed
1 teaspoon kosher salt
¼ teaspoon ground cumin
1 pinch smoked paprika
1 bunch baby-cut rainbow carrots
2 red or yellow endives
1 bunch radishes, greens still on
1 bunch broccolini
1 pound sugar snap peas
6 baby fennels
1 pint sweet cherry tomatoes

1. In a food processor, combine garlic, tahini, ⅓ cup of the olive oil, and lemon juice. Blend until smooth and airy. You may need to scrape the sides of the bowl a few times.

2. Add the chickpeas and puree, adding water if needed to help smooth it out.

3. When smooth, add salt and cumin, and puree again. Taste and add more salt if needed.

4. Move to a serving bowl and use the back of a spoon to create a divot or well in your hummus to hold the remaining 1 tablespoon of the olive oil. Add a pinch of smoked paprika around the well.

5. Wash, peel, and trim the vegetables, arranging them around a platter randomly to display their colors and shapes. Feel free to make substitutions for seasonality. Serve with the hummus.

BIERGARTEN SOFT PRETZELS AND SPICY HONEY MUSTARD

Nightcrawler turned me on to this little German place near Prospect Park that he likes to escape to when being a Krakoan delegate and an X-Man gets to be too much. We've been friends ever since we found ourselves in the crosshairs of the Punisher years ago. That's how you all make friends, right? Since then, it's been nice to kick back with a guy almost as agile as I am, just to roof-run and compare notes. (Hi, buddy, let's hang soon.) The important thing here is the pretzel, which is a soft and salty piece of the old country, and I'm thankful to Mr. Wagner for introducing me to it.

—Spider-Man

BIERGARTEN SOFT PRETZELS AND SPICY HONEY MUSTARD

Prep Time: 2 hours
V | **Yield:** 6 to 8 pretzels

PRETZELS:

1½ cups warm water

½ tablespoon dry active yeast

2 tablespoons brown sugar

4 cups bread flour

1 teaspoon kosher salt

3 tablespoons melted butter

1 egg

4 tablespoons baking soda

2 tablespoons coarse sea salt

HONEY MUSTARD DIP:

½ cup whole grain mustard

¼ cup spicy brown mustard

½ cup honey

½ cup mayonnaise

1 teaspoon turmeric powder

1 teaspoon chipotle powder

1. **TO MAKE THE PRETZELS:** Mix together the warm water, active yeast, and brown sugar until well dissolved and let sit 10 to 15 minutes or until the solution becomes foamy.

2. In a mixer, combine flour and 1 teaspoon of salt. Slowly mix in the foamy yeast solution, being sure to scrape the bowl and get all the love in.

3. Mix the dough and add in the melted butter. Dough will be messy. Empty onto a floured surface and knead until the dough comes together.

4. Place in a greased bowl and cover. Let rise in a warm place until it's doubled in size, approximately 1½ hours.

5. Preheat the oven to 400°F.

6. Once the dough has doubled, gently portion it into 6 to 8 equal pieces, depending on how big you like your pretzels.

7. Gently roll a portion of dough into a long log about ⅓ inch thick. Lay the log down and fold both ends over to make the pretzel shape. Set aside on an oiled parchment and repeat.

8. In a separate bowl, mix up 1 egg.

9. Bring 2 quarts of water and the baking soda to a simmer in a pot large enough to fully submerge a pretzel for blanching.

10. One at a time, dunk the pretzels fully in the water for about 30 to 40 seconds and remove to a toweled surface.

11. Brush the blanched pretzels with the beaten egg and sprinkle on sea salt.

12. Bake in the oven until golden, approximately 12 to 15 minutes. Keep in a warm place till serving.

13. **TO MAKE THE HONEY MUSTARD DIP:** In a small bowl, whisk together the mustards, honey, mayonnaise, turmeric, and chipotle powder. Serve on the side with your pretzels.

CEVICHE TIGERS MILK

You all might have heard that I've tangled with the Lizard dozens of times. It's possible I've vented to some of you on occasion, or generally complained about it at one point or another. So it's been established that I know him well enough to say he's a good guy underneath all those scales. It just takes getting him out from under that hard green exterior. This involves a lot of empathy, an open heart, and a formula I've developed to turn him back to his human form. But getting him to take it often poses a challenge. I got inventive one time and grabbed this ceviche dish from a Peruvian food cart owner. The Lizard might hate my antidote, but he loved the ceviche. And I quickly became a fan as well.

—Spider-Man

CEVICHE TIGERS MILK

Prep Time: Overnight, plus 2 hours
GF* | **Yield:** 4 portions

MARINADE:

1 cup fresh lime juice
½ cup fish stock, cold (gluten-free versions available, if preferred)
1 garlic clove
1 tablespoon cilantro stems (save leaves for garnish)
1 teaspoon kosher salt
2 tablespoons fresh chopped ginger
4 tablespoons ají amarillo paste

CEVICHE:

1 pound fluke or other firm sashimi-grade whitefish, cut into ⅓-inch-thick slices
¼ cup paper-thin-sliced red onion
1 large sweet potato, steamed, peeled, and small-diced (optional)
2 serrano chiles, sliced thin
4 teaspoons extra-virgin olive oil
½ cup corn nuts
½ bunch cilantro, stemmed
1 tablespoon flaky sea salt
4 lime wedges

1. Wrap a sweet potato in foil tightly and bake in a 350°F oven for 30 minutes. A fork should sink in easily, but the potato should not be shriveled or mushy. Cool, unwrapped, in the fridge overnight.

2. **TO MAKE THE MARINADE:** Blend lime juice, fish stock, garlic, cilantro stems, kosher salt, ginger, and ají amarillo paste together. Chill for an hour. Then strain through a fine sieve and set aside.

3. **TO MAKE THE CEVICHE:** In a medium mixing bowl on ice, add the sliced fish and onion. Cover with the fish stock marinade for at least 20 minutes before serving.

4. Spoon the ceviche into four small bowls, being sure to divide the fish, onion, and marinade equally between them.

5. Peel and dice your sweet potato. Then garnish with equal amounts of sweet potato, chiles, and olive oil.

6. Finish each bowl of the ceviche with corn nuts, cilantro leaf, a touch of sea salt, and a lime wedge.

ARAÑITAS

Rio outdid herself with this second dish. It's fried green plátano, as she'd say: plantains from her native Puerto Rico. They taste so good. I wish she would cook—um, I mean, I wish I could make them for myself every day. The fun part is that the name of this dish translates into "Little Spiders," so she thought it would be cute if she gave me this recipe.

—Spider-Man

ARAÑITAS

Prep Time: 20 minutes
V, V+*, GF | Yield: 4 servings

ARAÑITAS:

1 teaspoon kosher salt

2 large green plantains (note that yellow plantains will not work for this recipe)

Vegetable oil

DIPPING SAUCE (OPTIONAL):

½ cup mayonnaise (vegan versions available, if preferred)

⅓ cup ketchup

1 medium garlic clove, peeled and minced

½ teaspoon lime juice, plus more to taste

1 teaspoon kosher salt, plus more to taste

1 splash of your preferred hot sauce

1. **TO MAKE THE ARAÑITAS:** Fill a large bowl with cold water and add 1 teaspoon salt.

2. Peel the plantains by first cutting off both ends, then making three lengthwise slices through the skin. Carefully pull up the peel and remove it, starting at one of the corners with the edge of your fingernail or the tip of your knife. (Be careful: Plantain skins will stain your hands and clothing.)

3. Transfer whole plantains to the salt water and let sit for 5 to 10 minutes.

4. Pour enough vegetable oil to reach 3 inches in a large, deep skillet. Heat over medium-high heat until oil shimmers and reaches 350° to 375°F. You can test by adding a small piece of plantain; it will sizzle when the oil is hot enough.

5. **TO MAKE THE DIPPING SAUCE:** Combine mayonnaise, ketchup, garlic, lime juice, 1 teaspoon salt, and hot sauce. Mix well with a fork and refrigerate until ready to use.

6. Once oil is hot, remove the plantains from the water and dry very well with paper towels or a clean cloth. Grate the plantains on the large side of the grater, into a deep bowl.

7. Prepare a large plate or cookie sheet with paper towels. Use your fingers to pinch about 1 tablespoon of grated plantain and place into the palm of your hand. Use both hands to press the grated plantain flat; the starches in the plantain will help it stick together, so no need for an additional binder. Repeat until you've used up all the grated plantain.

8. One by one, carefully add grated plantain patties to the hot oil, using a splatter guard as needed to protect from splattering oil, being sure not to crowd the pan. Fry for 3 to 4 minutes total, flipping often to cook evenly.

9. Transfer to a paper towel–lined plate and sprinkle lightly with salt. Let cool for 1 minute (if you can wait that long), and eat immediately, dipping in mayo ketchup.

KRAVING VEGGIE DUMPLINGS

I've got to hand it to Sergei Kravinoff. He's meticulous, he's cunning, he's driven—and the goatee! Yeah, there'd be a lot to admire about Kraven the Hunter if it weren't for the whole hunter part. Oh and the fact that I'm usually his prey. I mean the man wears a lion-themed ensemble, yet somehow this decidedly furless Spider jumps to the top of his list of big game? I'll put it to you this way. After the first time I tussled with Mr. Lion Pelt's nets, traps, and chiseled jawline, I swore off meat for a month. Fortunately, there was a spot in Astoria that made my favorite dumplings in a veggie variety. I became such a regular that they offered to let me pinch my own dumplings together before they cooked them for me. Note: I had them include detailed instructions on this technique, reproduced below. They offered to name the dumplings after me on the menu, but I thought the best revenge would be for them to name them after Kraven.

—Spider-Man

KRAVING VEGGIE DUMPLINGS

Prep Time: 1 hour
V | Yield: 16 dumplings

DUMPLINGS:

3 tablespoons olive oil

1 tablespoon minced ginger

1 tablespoon minced scallion whites

1 teaspoon minced garlic

½ cup thinly sliced shiitake mushrooms

8 ounces tightly packed spinach

½ teaspoon sesame oil

2 teaspoons soy sauce

Salt and freshly ground pepper, to taste

1 tablespoon cornstarch

1 pack of 16 white, round dumpling wrappers (look for eggless options to make vegan)

4 tablespoons water

SAUCE:

2 tablespoons black vinegar

2 tablespoons soy sauce

1 tablespoon finely julienned ginger

1. **TO MAKE THE DUMPLINGS:** In a medium nonstick pan heat 2 tablespoons of olive oil. Then add the minced ginger, scallion whites, and garlic. Sauté until fragrant and tender. Add the shiitake mushrooms and sauté until fully cooked.

2. Add the spinach; it will quickly wilt. Season with sesame oil and the soy sauce. Remove from heat, spread on a tray or plate, and place in the fridge or freezer to rapidly cool.

3. When the filling is cool, drain the excess liquid and put it in a food processor. Pulse until the filling is roughly chopped and easily stays together when pressed. Season with salt and pepper.

4. To prepare your wrapping station, dust a tray with a bit of cornstarch to prevent the dumplings from sticking. Fill a bowl with a bit of water.

5. Start small, adding just a bit of filling in the center of your first wrapper. Wet the edges with your finger gently and close the wrapper around the filling, crimping as you go. The edges should meet in the center, creating the look of a pouch. Then go back around, pressing with two fingers at each fold to make sure it's fully sealed.

6. Alternative method: If you prefer a simpler approach, instead just fold over the wrapper and seal in a half-moon. You can start with a half-moon that has a couple of creases and add more as you make more dumplings and feel more confident.

7. Set aside on the dusted tray until ready to cook.

8. Once ready, place your dumplings in a nonstick pan evenly spaced with a tablespoon of oil and 4 tablespoons of water. Cover and cook on medium-high heat to steam until dumplings start to crisp up. Remove the lid and cook until golden on the underside. You can also boil water and drop the dumplings in and cook them until they float. Just be gentle and careful that you don't break them open. Do a test first in either case.

9. **TO MAKE THE SAUCE:** Combine the black vinegar, soy sauce, and ginger and serve the dumplings on the side.

CHEESE AREPAS

Thinking back to our roots together, my first recipe ties back to when I had just sold my first set of Spidey pics to J. Jonah Jameson. My first job, my first paying gig. I was thrilled, and rich (I thought). I was so ecstatic that I got off at the wrong train stop on my way home and ended up in East Elmhurst. Right in front of a Colombian restaurant that seemed to be calling to me. I answered the call and ordered this cheese dish on a lark. Good choice, Parker—it served as the capper to an amazing day. It became a bit of a tradition to stop by there during high school, either to celebrate selling more photos or to drown my sorrows when I didn't make the sale. Cheese Arepas, my inner artist's comfort food and some of Queens's Finest.

—Spider-Man

CHEESE AREPAS

Prep Time: 20 minutes
V, GF | **Yield:** 6 to 8 arepas

2 cups milk or water
2 cups masarepa
1 teaspoon kosher salt
¾ pound shredded mozzarella
2 tablespoons unsalted butter
2 tablespoons canola oil

1. Combine the milk, masarepa, and salt in a bowl and mix well. Then stir in a quarter of the shredded mozzarella.

2. Portion your mix into sixteen golf-ball-size spheres.

3. Place one ball into a sandwich bag and press down, forming a flat disk. Set your disk aside and repeat, using the same sandwich bag, until you have 16 disks.

4. Apply the remaining cheese evenly across the top of eight of your sixteen disks.

5. Cover each of your cheesy disks with one of the eight opposing halves. If needed, use more water to get them sticky enough to seal by gently pressing all the way around the edge of the circle. You should have 8 white burger-patty-looking pucks at the end.

6. Melt the butter with canola oil on a griddle or skillet, then reduce to medium-low heat. Cook each arepa until golden on both sides, carefully turning until it's done. This should take about 3 to 4 minutes per side. To test if your arepas are fully cooked, tear one open slightly to confirm that the cheese is fully melted.

PIEROGIS

RED & BLACK: I got this recipe off the Rhino during a team-up I had with him in Red Hook.
RED & BLUE: Excuse me, did you just say the Rhino?
RED & BLACK: Yeah, Aleksei's a sweetheart.
RED & BLUE: Um, sure, when he's not trying to shish kebab yours truly with that horn of his.
RED & BLACK: C'mon, man, he's great. And tells the best stories about his childhood and how his little old "babushka" would make these amazing pierogis for him as a treat to make him feel better when he would get in trouble at school.
RED & BLUE: You keep interesting company, kid. But thanks for your help, I'll handle the rest of Brooklyn, if you'll take care of jdshfkdshfdkjhaskdjh . . .

Our recording got cut off here, for, reasons . . . But we picked up long enough for the kid to share the following.

39

PIEROGIS

Prep Time: 2 hours
V | Yield: 50 to 60 pierogis

DOUGH:

1 cup whole milk
2 tablespoons canola oil
1 egg
3½ cups all-purpose flour

FILLING:

2 pounds potatoes
4 tablespoons unsalted butter
2 cups small-diced sweet onion
1 teaspoon kosher salt
1 teaspoon freshly ground black pepper
½ cup farmer cheese
1 bunch dill, chopped
1 cup sour cream
1 cup applesauce

SPECIAL TOOL:

3-inch-diameter cookie cutter

1. Peel 2 pounds of potatoes and cut them into 2-inch chunks. Cover with cold water in a pot and bring to a simmer on high.

2. When cold water comes to a simmer, at about 20 to 30 minutes, the potatoes will be pretty close to being done. To test, see if they just break up with a fork.

3. Drain the potatoes and mash well in a bowl or pot with a whisk or potato masher, leaving no lumps. Set aside.

4. **TO MAKE THE DOUGH:** Mix the milk, canola oil, and egg in a bowl. Slowly stream this into a mixer filled with the flour.

5. When mixed, remove the dough from the mixer and onto a floured surface. Knead for 3 to 5 minutes, until a smooth ball is formed. Add more flour or water as you go, if necessary. Place in an oiled bowl, cover with plastic wrap, and chill in the fridge for 30 minutes.

6. While your dough is chilling, take out a large pan and sauté the onions with butter until golden. Season with salt and pepper.

7. **TO MAKE THE FILLING:** In a mixing bowl, combine half of the sautéed onions with the mashed potatoes and farmer cheese. Mix well and season with salt and pepper if needed. Reserve at room temperature.

8. Put a large pot of salted water on to boil.
9. Take the pierogi dough from the fridge and roll out on a floured surface, as thin as you can without it tearing. If it's easier, you can do this using part of the dough at a time. Once spread thin, use a 3-inch diameter cookie cutter to punch out rounds.
10. Fill the dough rounds with about a tablespoon of potato filling each. Seal the dumplings by wetting your fingers with water and pinching the edges.

11. In batches, cook the dumplings in the boiling water. Remove them when they float and the dough is fully cooked, around 2 to 3 minutes per batch. You can keep them hot on a buttered tray until they are all cooked.

12. If you want to take an extra step, sauté them in butter until they start to turn golden.

13. Serve the pierogis on a plate topped with chopped dill and sides of sour cream, applesauce, and the remaining half of the sautéed onion.

CHEESE KNISHES

Being a New York–based hero, it's not all laser battles and high-speed chases through Midtown. Sometimes it's as simple and perfect as finding a good perch to take it all in. A good one is at the south end of Borough Park while the sun goes down. From my vantage point, it's the best view in the world. And sometimes that moment of sky-high Zen is complemented by a kind older woman offering you a plate of freshly made potato treats from her windowsill. I really was hanging outside the sixth-story window of Edith's Brooklyn brownstone. I think it says a lot that she offered the strange masked man some food instead of throwing a shoe at me, or a book, or a lamp or a—well, you get the idea. That's the thing about New Yorkers, they're always ready to lend a helping hand. Even if they rarely have a word of small talk to spare. Now that we've gotten to know each other, Edith talks about her kids, her grandkids, and her husband, Jude. I tell her about my day. Now I swing by whenever I can, not just for the food, but for the conversation. She gave me this recipe with her blessing, but on the condition that I stop leaving footprints on her sill. Fair deal.

—Spider-Man

CHEESE KNISHES

Prep Time: Overnight, plus 2 hours
V | **Yield:** 20 knishes

DOUGH:

2 cups all-purpose flour, plus more for dusting
1 teaspoon kosher salt
1 teaspoon baking powder
3 eggs
3 tablespoons canola oil

FILLING:

2 cups cottage cheese
½ cup cream cheese
½ cup granulated sugar
1 vanilla bean, scraped
1 lemon, zested
1 egg yolk
2 tablespoons water

SERVE:

One 8-ounce jar cherry jam

1. The night before, set a strainer in a bowl and drain the cottage cheese in it. Keep everything in the fridge overnight.

2. **TO MAKE THE DOUGH:** Combine flour, salt, and baking powder in a mixer.

3. In a separate bowl, whisk eggs and canola oil together, then stream into the flour mix.

4. Remove everything from the mixer and kneed on a flour-covered surface for 5 to 8 minutes, until smooth and

elastic. Depending on the moisture, you may need to add flour as you go. Cover with plastic wrap and let rest for 30 minutes in the fridge.

5. Preheat your oven to 375°F.

6. **TO MAKE THE FILLING:** Combine the strained cottage cheese, cream cheese, sugar, scraped vanilla bean seeds, and lemon zest in a clean bowl in the mixer. Set aside.

7. Remove the dough from the fridge and cut it in half. Leaving one half covered in plastic so it doesn't dry out, roll out the other half on a flour-covered surface to about $1/16$ of an inch. Cut this into 3-inch squares, and dust them all with flour. Then do the same with the other half of your dough. When finished, set aside covered. The squares will shrink a bit, but you should be able to stretch them back out when you fill them.

8. Taking the first dough square, add 1 tablespoon of filling to the center and bring the corners of the square up and form a pouch. Seal it shut, wetting your fingers under water if necessary, and place it on a parchment-lined baking tray. Repeat until all the squares are filled and sealed.

9. In a separate bowl, combine the egg yolk with 2 tablespoons of water. Brush this mix onto each knish and then bake them until golden, about 15 to 20 minutes.

10. Serve them warm with a side of cherry jam.

CASSAVA FRIES

While the Western world prefers potatoes for making fries, in Wakanda we utilize the magnificent cassava. You can find fried cassava root at outdoor markets across the country and it is often served in Wakandan homes for every meal. Try serving these with spiced ketchup. These were definitely a dish that young T'Challa and Shuri enjoyed with their breakfast eggs.

—Ndi Chikondi

Executive Chef, Royal Palace of Wakanda

CASSAVA FRIES

Prep Time: 5 minutes | **Cook Time:** 5 minutes
V, V+, GF | **Yield:** 4 to 6 servings

3 pounds cassava root, also known as yuca
2 cups vegetable oil
Kosher salt, to taste

SPECIAL TOOL:
Dutch oven

1. Cut the ends off the cassava, peel, and cut out the core.
2. Cut the cassava into 2-inch pieces.
3. Heat oil in the Dutch oven to 350°F.
4. Fry the cassava pieces until golden on each side, about 3 to 5 minutes.
5. Remove from oil with a slotted spoon. Dry and drain on paper towels. Salt to taste.

CHARRED OKURU

Okuru, or okra, as it is known in English, is seen across the continent of Africa and is used in many different dishes. This is a simple recipe that quickly cooks the okra in boiling water and then finishes them over an open flame. This is a great appetizer when served on skewers with dipping sauces like curried aioli or muhammara.

—Ndi Chikondi
Executive Chef, Royal Palace of Wakanda

CHARRED OKURU

Prep Time: 5 minutes
V, V+, GF | **Yield:** 10 servings

One 12-ounce package fresh whole okra
2 tablespoons peanut oil
1 tablespoon nutritional yeast
Salt and freshly ground pepper, to taste
1 lemon, for garnish

SPECIAL TOOL:
Grill

1. Blanch okra in a large stockpot of salted boiling water for 2 minutes.
2. Transfer to a medium-sized mixing bowl and toss the okra with the peanut oil.
3. Cook okra over a hot grill until each side has grill marks and a little char.
4. Transfer back to the mixing bowl and toss with nutritional yeast. Salt and pepper to taste.
5. Serve with lemon wedges.

PLANTAIN CHIPS

For those of us Wakandans that travel, we enjoy dining at restaurants that feature foods from the African diaspora. There is a Jamaican restaurant in Brooklyn that features many of the same flavors as Wakanda food. The Dora Milajae and I often enjoy visiting and ordering the plantain chips. They are long and thin and crispy and are often served with a variety of dips and salsas.

—Ndi Chikondi
Executive Chef, Royal Palace of Wakanda

PLANTAIN CHIPS

Prep Time: 5 minutes | **Cook Time:** 5 minutes
V, V+, GF | **Yield:** 4 to 6 servings

4 green plantains
2 cups vegetable oil
Kosher salt

SPECIAL TOOL:
Cast-iron skillet or Dutch oven

1. Cut off the ends of the plantains and peel.
2. Using a vegetable peeler or mandoline, slice the plantains thinly lengthwise.
3. In a cast-iron skillet or Dutch oven, heat the oil to 350°F.
4. Drop the slices of plantains into the hot oil, about 3 to 4 at a time.
5. Fry the slices until they become crispy and golden brown on both sides, about 1 to 2 minutes.
6. Remove from oil and drain on paper towels.
7. Season with salt.

OKRA FRITTERS

The okra fritters were one of the most popular items on the family food-stand menu from before I was born. Fritters are commonly seen throughout Wakanda and this version uses two of the country's greatest crops, okra and corn.

—Ndi Chikondi
Executive Chef, Royal Palace of Wakanda

OKRA FRITTERS

Prep Time: 10 minutes | **Cook Time:** 10 minutes
V | **Yield:** 4 servings

1 egg
¼ cup goat's milk (or whole cow's milk)
½ cup all-purpose flour
¼ cup cornmeal
1 teaspoon garlic powder
1 teaspoon smoked paprika
1 teaspoon onion powder
1 teaspoon kosher salt
1 teaspoon freshly ground black pepper
1 cup thinly sliced fresh okra (or frozen okra pieces, thawed)
1 cup corn kernels
2 cups vegetable oil

1. In a medium mixing bowl, whisk the egg with goat's milk.
2. In a separate bowl, combine flour, cornmeal, garlic powder, smoked paprika, onion powder, salt, and pepper.
3. Pour egg mixture into flour mixture and mix with a spatula.
4. Fold in the okra and corn.
5. Heat oil in a large skillet to 325°F.
6. Using a large soupspoon, drop spoonfuls of the batter into the hot oil. Use a slotted spoon or spatula to turn the fritters until they are brown on all sides, about 2 to 3 minutes.
7. Remove from oil and cool on paper towels.

HARISSA-SPICED POPCORN

Although education and learning were heavily pushed in the Royal Palace, when Princess Shuri and King T'Challa were young children, they were granted movie nights from time to time. They always watched the newest films on the newest screening equipment that was being tested. On those evenings I would use our air popper and make them this treat. I would serve it with the homemade tamarind cola. This popcorn recipe has been modified for popping the kernels over a common home stove.

—Ndi Chikondi
Executive Chef, Royal Palace of Wakanda

HARISSA-SPICED POPCORN

Cook Time: 10 minutes
V, GF | **Yield:** 4 servings

POPCORN:
1 cup coconut oil
⅓ cup popcorn kernels
1 tablespoon Harissa Spice Mix
1 tablespoon nutritional yeast
1 teaspoon kosher salt

HARISSA SPICE MIX:
1 tablespoon chile powder
1 tablespoon smoked paprika
1 tablespoon ground cumin
1 tablespoon ground caraway
1 tablespoon ground fennel
1 tablespoon garlic powder
1 tablespoon ground coriander
1 tablespoon freshly ground black pepper
1 tablespoon ground cinnamon
1 tablespoon ground ginger
1 tablespoon dried mint
1 tablespoon dried parsley

1. Melt coconut oil in a thick-bottomed medium-sized saucepan on medium-high heat.

2. Pour the kernels into the pot and cover. As the kernels begin to pop gently, shake the pan holding on to the lid. As the popping starts to slow down, remove the pot from heat.

3. In a small mixing bowl combine Harissa Spice Mix, nutritional yeast, and salt.

4. Toss the popped kernels with the spices.

BOILED MTEDZA

Boiling mtedza, or groundnuts, such as peanuts, is very inherently African. You will find this preparation all across Wakanda. I was shocked to learn that boiled peanuts can be found throughout the world. After some research I discovered that it was the enslaved Africans who were brought to America that also brought with them this tradition of boiling groundnuts. This snack is best enjoyed with a tamarind cola.

—Ndi Chikondi

Executive Chef, Royal Palace of Wakanda

BOILED MTEDZA

Cook Time: 10 minutes
V, GF | Yield: 4 servings

1 pound raw or dried peanuts in shells
6 curry leaves
3 tablespoons kosher salt
Water to cover peanuts, about 12 cups

1. Rinse the peanuts in a strainer and transfer to a large stockpot.

2. Add curry leaves, salt, and water.

3. Cover and bring to a boil over high heat.

4. Reduce heat to medium and simmer covered until the peanuts are soft, about 3 hours.

5. Remove the pot from heat and strain the peanuts.

6. Enjoy them warm or chilled. To eat, pinch one end of the shell to pop out the peanut flesh. Some people also like to slurp the liquid in the shell. Discard the shell and repeat.

7. The peanuts can be stored refrigerated for up to 6 days.

ZOUMA BOWA

The Dora Milaje were regular customers at my family's market food stand. Eventually Anti Bahiya began to curate snacks for them when traveling and training. She created these smoked, marinated, and then dehydrated mushrooms to resemble a Western-style meat jerky. They are a tasty snack for anytime but especially if you find yourself out in the woods for a while.

—Ndi Chikondi
Executive Chef, Royal Palace of Wakanda

ZOUMA BOWA

Prep Time: 10 minutes | **Cook Time:** 5 hours
V | **Yield:** 1 pint

1 cup soy sauce
1 cup water
¼ cup rice wine vinegar
½ cup brown sugar
1 tablespoon onion powder
1 tablespoon garlic powder
1 teaspoon freshly ground black pepper
2 pints mushrooms (lion's mane, shiitake, oyster, or pioppini)

SPECIAL TOOLS:
Dehydrator
Smoker
Vacuum sealer

1. **TO MAKE THE MARINADE:** In a medium-sized saucepan, bring the soy sauce, water, rice vinegar, brown sugar, onion powder, garlic powder, and black pepper up to a boil over medium-high heat. Once boiling, remove from heat and cool down.

2. **TO MAKE THE MUSHROOMS:** Trim the mushrooms into small clusters and clean off dirt.

3. Smoke mushrooms according to your smoker's directions for 5 to 10 minutes depending on their size, being sure not to cook them but just incorporate the smoke smell. Remove from heat and cool.

4. Place mushrooms in a vacuum seal bag, pour in the marinade, and marinate overnight. If you don't have a vacuum sealer, place mushrooms in a 1-gallon ziplock bag and pour double the amount of marinade on top. Marinate refrigerated overnight, but no more than 2 days.

5. Drain the mushrooms and place in a dehydrator set for 145°F. Let the mushrooms dry out for 3 to 5 hours. They should be chewy and a little tough but not crunchy.

6. Store in an airtight container for up to 2 weeks.

VEGETABLE SAMOSAS

Samosas truly are a delicious and versatile snack. This meatless version includes peas and some vegetable stock and curry powder to spice up the rest of the vegetables. I have modified this recipe to use spring roll wrappers because in all my travels and tasting of samosas, I love a crispy crust the best.

—Ndi Chikondi
Executive Chef, Royal Palace of Wakanda

VEGETABLE SAMOSAS

Prep Time: 10 minutes | **Cook Time:** 20 minutes
V | Yield: 2 to 4 servings

1 tablespoon peanut oil
1 medium carrot, small diced
2 celery stalks, small diced
1 small yellow onion, small diced
2 small russet potatoes, small diced
2 cups peas
1 cup vegetable stock
¼ cup lemon juice
2 tablespoons yellow curry powder
1 teaspoon ground ginger
1 teaspoon freshly ground black pepper
1 teaspoon crushed chiles
1 teaspoon onion powder
2 teaspoons garlic powder
1 tablespoon salt
2 bay leaves
20 sheets of 5-inch spring roll pastry wrappers
Water for sealing wrappers
2 cups vegetable oil

1. In a medium saucepan, heat peanut oil over medium heat. Add carrot, celery, onion, and potatoes. Cook for 4 minutes, stirring occasionally.

2. Add peas, vegetable stock, lemon juice, curry powder, ground ginger, black pepper, chiles, onion powder, garlic powder, salt, and bay leaves. Mix together in the pan, cover, and simmer for 10 minutes.

3. Remove filling from heat, transfer to a baking pan to cool, and remove the bay leaves.
4. To fold the samosas, cut each spring roll wrapper into 3 equal rectangles going vertically. Stack the rectangles and cover with a damp paper towel while folding to keep the wrappers from drying out.
5. Take the first rectangle piece and place it on a cutting board horizontally. Take the bottom right corner of the rectangle and fold it across to the left to form the first triangle for the pocket for the filling.
6. Take the top of the new triangle and fold it down and across to the left, aligning it with the flat bottom, making a new layer for the pocket.
7. Pick up the wrapper pocket and spoon in 1 tablespoon of filling.
8. Fold the pocket across to the left again, leaving a short rectangle. To seal off the wrapper, pat a small amount of water on the end and fold over. Repeat until you have used up all the filling.
9. To cook the samosas, heat vegetable oil in a frying pan to 350°F. Fry the samosas until brown on each side, about 3 minutes.

SHRIMP CEVICHE

Let's face it—no matter how many tutorial pages we include about frying safety, some folks just aren't capable of crispifying their food without also ending up covered in burns so severe that they make my skin look as smooth as a newborn baby's behind. For those unfortunate few, I invented a special nonfried variation that allows for the same delicious fillings you can find inside a chimi, with only a fraction of the danger. If you're feeling really fancy, try this ceviche. It is culinary perfection, in a chimi and on its own.

—Deadpool

SHRIMP CEVICHE

Prep Time: 1 hour
GF | Yield: 6 servings

¼ cup fresh lime juice
¼ cup fresh lemon juice
1 pound shrimp, peeled and deveined, cooked and chopped
2 tablespoons olive oil
1 red onion, diced
2 Roma tomatoes, cored, seeded, and diced
1 avocado, peeled, pitted, and diced
1 to 2 jalapeños or serrano chiles, seeded and diced
½ cup loosely packed fresh cilantro leaves, chopped
Salt and freshly ground black pepper
Limes, for garnish
Chips or fried corn tortillas, for serving

1. In a large serving bowl, combine the lime and lemon juice. Toss the shrimp in the juice. Cover, refrigerate, and marinate for 1 hour. After 1 hour, drain the shrimp, put them back in the bowl, and mix in the rest of the ingredients.

2. Give the ceviche an extra squeeze of fresh lime right before serving and garnish with lime wedges. Serve with chips or fried corn tortillas.

NEGASONIC WARHEADS

Do you ever get tired of this thing we call life? Ever wonder why we bother when nothing we do actually matters? Well, put away the black eyeliner, Nietzsche, because Uncle Wade is about to get all X-istential on you. See, we're not all players in some big cosmic game, no matter what the Watcher tries to tell you. We all carve our own paths in this miserable existence, and mine happens to be an extremely lucrative one based entirely on making mayhem for money! But that doesn't mean I don't find myself getting a little numb to the world every now and then. On those occasions, I pop a few of these blazing hot bacon-wrapped stuffed jalapeños—named in honor of my favorite emo mutant, Negasonic Teenage Warhead—into my world-famous word-hole. Because I'm human(-ish), too, and sometimes I just need to feel something real.

—Deadpool

NEGASONIC WARHEADS

Prep Time: 5 minutes | **Cook Time:** 35 to 40 minutes
GF | **Yield:** 20 peppers

1 cup (8 ounces) cream cheese, softened
1 cup grated pepper Jack
1 teaspoon chile powder
½ teaspoon cayenne pepper
2 shallots, minced
10 straight, similarly sized jalapeños, halved lengthwise and seeded
20 cocktail sausages
20 bacon slices
(about 2 packs)

1. Preheat the oven to 375°F. Set a wire rack over a baking sheet.

2. In a small bowl, mix the cream cheese, pepper Jack, spices, and minced shallots until well combined.

3. Spread 1 tablespoon of the cheese mixture on each jalapeño slice until it is completely covered and top with a mini sausage. Wrap a slice of bacon around the filled jalapeño, covering it from end to end so the bacon overlaps slightly. If necessary, secure with a toothpick.

4. Place the jalapeños on the rack in the baking sheet. Bake for 35 to 40 minutes, until bacon is crisp and jalapeños are soft.

CHICK-ARRONES

Anyone who's ever met me knows I tend to push everything in my life to the extreme. My fighting style. My sense of humor. My complete and utter lack of social graces. But even I'm self-aware enough to admit that, after a while, "extreme" doesn't seem quite so extreme anymore. When you're expected to push boundaries all the time, suddenly pushing boundaries becomes the expected. And that's the opposite of edgy. Luckily, your old pal Deadpool wasn't about to be left in the dust as a new generation of trendsetters and tastemakers pushed the envelope in different directions. So I locked myself in a motel room for three weeks and tried to think of the most over-the-top idea to help me reclaim my rightful place as the champion of excess. The answer came to me in a moment of pure cosmic awareness. Chicken nachos—but get this: The nachos are the chicken. Mind. Blown. To the extreme!

—Deadpool

CHICK-ARRONES

Prep Time: 15 minutes | **Cook Time:** 20 minutes
Yield: 4 servings

2 boneless, skinless chicken breasts
1 teaspoon paprika
¼ teaspoon cayenne pepper
Salt and freshly ground black pepper
½ cup milk
½ cup sour cream
1½ cups all-purpose flour
1 cup yellow cornmeal
4 tablespoons cornstarch
1 teaspoon garlic powder
Oil, such as peanut, vegetable, or canola, for frying

1. Holding a knife parallel to the cutting board, slice each chicken breast in half lengthwise. Place a piece of chicken between 2 pieces of parchment paper, and pound with a mallet until about ½ inch thick. Cut the chicken into "chip"-sized triangles. Repeat with remaining pieces of chicken.

2. Whisk paprika, cayenne pepper, salt and pepper (to taste), milk, and sour cream in a large bowl, and add chicken to marinate while you work on the next step.

3. Prepare the dredge by whisking flour, cornmeal, cornstarch, 1 teaspoon salt, and garlic powder together in a shallow dish. Set aside.

4. In a large, deep skillet, heat 2 inches of oil to 365°F (you can also use a deep fryer). Working in small batches, remove the chicken pieces from the marinade, letting the excess drip off before rolling each piece through the dredge until completely coated. Fry the chicken "chips" in the hot oil, turning regularly, until all sides are golden brown. Place on a wire rack or paper towel to drain, and sprinkle with more salt if desired.

I'M A REAL FUNGI

As you may have noticed, I wear a mask. Why is that, you ask? Am I trying to hide my true identity to protect the people I love? Nah. All the people I love are totally capable of protecting themselves. It's because my face has been so ravaged by disease that my healing factor can barely keep it in check! Still hungry? Good. If you still have an appetite after that disgusting truth, then you'll probably enjoy these less-than-lovely little mushrooms. They may be wrinkled and ugly, like my face, but they're also buttery and irresistible, like my soul. It's what's on the inside that matters these days, right, ladies? So time to stop judging a book by its cover (unless it's this book, which you already bought, so I trust your judgment), and give these fungi a chance!

—Deadpool

I'M A REAL FUNGI

Cook Time: 10 minutes
V | Yield: 20 to 30 mushrooms

2 tablespoons olive oil
3 tablespoons salted butter
8 cloves garlic, minced
1½ pounds whole mushrooms, cleaned and stemmed (stems reserved)
Salt, to taste
¼ to ½ teaspoon red pepper flakes, depending on heat preference
¼ cup vermouth
Crusty bread, for serving

1. In a large sauté pan on medium heat, combine olive oil and butter until the butter begins to foam. Add garlic, and sauté until just translucent. Add the mushroom caps and stems, and cook, stirring only occasionally, until the mushrooms are brown and have absorbed most of the butter. Add the salt, red pepper flakes, and vermouth, using the liquid to deglaze the pan.

2. Cook for about 5 minutes, then remove from heat. Serve hot with crusty bread for sopping up the sauce.

STREET-CORNER STREET CORN

When you're in a line of work like mine, danger lurks around almost every corner. But on the corners where danger doesn't lurk, hopefully there's some sort of food cart selling local specialties. Eating street food is a lot like being a mercenary, actually. One wrong choice, and you could end up crawling your way into the nearest hospital with a hole in your gut. One dish that never did me wrong was the Mexican street corn sold just across the street from the hidden Hydra warehouse near the docks. (You remember the one.) Unfortunately, after I burned the warehouse down with everyone inside, it really put a damper on the daily lunch rush, and the cart went out of business. Fortunately, I was able to whip up this off-the-cob variation in memory of the fallen.

—Deadpool

STREET-CORNER STREET CORN

Prep Time: 5 minutes | **Cook Time:** 5 minutes
V | **Yield:** About 8 serving

DRESSING:

½ cup mayonnaise
2 tablespoons chopped chipotle peppers in adobo sauce
1 cup crumbled cotija cheese, divided

CORN:

2 tablespoons olive oil
2 tablespoons unsalted butter
3 cloves garlic, minced
1 serrano chile, seeded and minced
2 teaspoons kosher salt
One 32-ounce package frozen corn, defrosted
Juice of 1 lime

1. **TO MAKE THE DRESSING:** Combine the mayonnaise, chile, and ½ cup of the cotija in a small bowl. Set aside.

2. **TO MAKE THE CORN:** Heat a large sauté pan on medium, and add olive oil, swirling to coat the pan. Melt butter in the pan. When the butter begins to foam, add garlic, serrano chile, and salt, and sauté until tender. Add corn and cook, stirring constantly, for about 5 minutes or until warmed through. Add the lime juice and stir to combine.

3. Transfer the corn to a large bowl and mix in the prepared dressing. Sprinkle with the remaining cotija before serving.

POOL-TINE

Oh, Canada! My home and native land! If you're in the mood for some authentic cuisine from the Great White North, look no further than poutine—the semiofficial national dish of a nation that, for some unknown reason, still refuses to acknowledge me as its most valuable export. Poutine, which roughly translates to "face full of yum" in Saskatchewanian, consists of a heaping pile of golden brown pommes frites (French fries to you Yankees), smothered in a rich brown gravy and topped off with cheese curds. If that sounds like a heart attack on a plate to you, you're right. But if your internal compass is set to deliciousness, then poutine is true north! (If you can't find quality cheese curds, you can sub in mozzarella pearls instead, but your visa will instantly be revoked. Sorry.)

—Deadpool

POOL-TINE

Prep Time: 5 minutes | **Cook Time:** 45 minutes
V | **Yield:** 6 servings

POTATOES:

3 pounds russet (or other baking) potatoes, cut into wedges
Scant ¼ cup olive oil, to coat
Kosher salt

GRAVY:

2 cups vegetable broth
2 cups water
2 teaspoons beef bouillon
4 tablespoons (½ stick) salted butter
4 cloves garlic, minced
1 shallot, minced
6 tablespoons all-purpose flour
1 tablespoon Worcestershire sauce
½ teaspoon kosher salt
Freshly ground black pepper, to taste

SERVE:

One 8-ounce package fresh mozzarella pearls or cheese curds
Fresh parsley, for garnish (optional)

1. Line 2 rimmed baking sheets with parchment paper and place them in the oven. Preheat the oven to 450°F.

2. **TO MAKE THE POTATOES:** Rinse the potato wedges to remove the excess starch, and pat dry. In a large mixing bowl, coat the potatoes in olive oil and salt to taste. Carefully add the potatoes to the baking sheets in a single layer, being careful not to overcrowd the pan.

3. Bake the potatoes for 20 minutes. Remove the sheets from the oven, shake them to turn potatoes, and bake another 10 to 15 minutes, until crisp and brown.

4. **TO MAKE THE GRAVY:** Combine the broth, water, and bouillon in a medium bowl, and set aside.

5. In the meantime, melt the butter on medium heat in a medium saucepan. Add the minced garlic and shallot and cook until translucent. Add the flour, and continue to cook, stirring continuously until the roux turns a deep golden brown.

6. Slowly add the broth mixture, stirring until smooth. Add Worcestershire sauce and salt and continue to cook on medium heat until the gravy thickens.
7. To assemble your Pool-Tine, place your crispy fries in a bowl, sprinkle with mozzarella pearls or cheese curds, top with gravy, season with pepper to taste, and top with parsley, if desired.

FIREBALLS

While I've somehow become known for carrying a wide variety of weapons, I'll be honest: For a guy with a job as deadly as mine, I actually prefer to play it safe. I mean, who needs an Infinity Gauntlet when the classics—like guns and swords—get the job done in a much simpler and less world-shattering way. But on the occasions when I do have to pull out the heavy artillery, there are few weapons more singularly satisfying than a flamethrower. After a long day of scorching the eyebrows off Hydra agents, I find myself craving something that will make me sweat as much on the inside as I do on the outside. That's where these little Buffalo chicken meatballs come in. While the blue cheese center cools them down a bit, you should still use caution. These balls have some real kick!

—Deadpool

FIREBALLS

Prep Time: 1 hour 10 minutes | **Cook Time:** 6 to 8 minutes
Yield: 18 balls

FILLING:

⅓ cup (2 ounces) crumbled blue cheese

¼ cup finely diced celery

BALLS:

4 tablespoons (½ stick) salted butter, melted

4 tablespoons hot sauce of your choice

½ teaspoon kosher salt

Freshly ground black pepper, to taste

1 teaspoon baking powder

1 pound ground chicken

½ cup all-purpose flour

DREDGING:

2 eggs

2 tablespoons hot sauce

1 cup all-purpose flour

1 teaspoon kosher salt

Freshly ground black pepper, to taste

Peanut or canola oil, for frying

SAUCE:

½ cup hot sauce

3 tablespoons honey

2 tablespoons ketchup

4 tablespoons (½ stick) salted butter

1. Line a baking sheet with foil or parchment, and set aside.
2. **TO MAKE THE FILLING:** Combine blue cheese and celery in a small bowl and set aside.
3. **TO MAKE THE BALLS:** In a medium bowl, mix melted butter, hot sauce, salt, pepper, and baking powder. Add ground chicken to mixture and work it with your hands until well combined. Sprinkle flour over the mixture and work again until incorporated. Using a spoon or your fingers, scoop 2 tablespoons of chicken mixture and make an indent in the meat with your thumb. Add a pinch of the filling to the indent and form the meat into a ball around the filling. Set on baking sheet and repeat until all the mixture is used. Place the baking sheet in the refrigerator to chill for at least 1 hour.

4. **TO PREPARE YOUR DREDGING STATIONS AND FRY:**
   Beat the eggs with 2 tablespoons of hot sauce in a small bowl, and mix the flour, salt, and pepper in a separate one. When you're ready to fry, heat about 2 inches of oil in a large heavy-bottomed skillet or frying pan to 365°F (a deep fryer can be used as well). Working in small batches, dredge each ball in the egg mixture, followed by the flour mixture, and then add to the hot oil. Fry each batch until the balls are a deep golden-brown color and cooked through, 3 to 4 minutes. Drain on a wire rack or paper towels.

5. **TO MAKE THE SAUCE:**
   Combine all the ingredients in a small saucepan on medium heat until smooth and hot.

6. Serve the Fireballs with the sauce on the side for dipping.

BULGING MUSSELS

If you happened to be a super-powered individual in the '90s, you saw your fair share of impressive muscles. And I'm not talking about your typical, everyday, super-hero-wrapped-in-a-form-fitting-spandex-costume muscles. No, no, no! I'm referring to hulking physiques so overexaggerated that you could make out every strained strand of sinew through a full suit of body armor! It was a weird time, kids. Thankfully, anatomy seems to have toned itself back down a bit in the decades that followed, and we're all better off for it. But while the days of giant muscles on the battlefield may be far behind us, the days of giant mussels, steamed and served in a vegetable broth and cream sauce, will hopefully never end.

—Deadpool

BULGING MUSSELS

Cook Time: 10 to 15 minutes
Yield: 6 servings

1 to 2 tablespoons oil, for pan
2 tablespoons salted butter
2 garlic cloves, minced
½ cup fine breadcrumbs
½ cup vegetable broth
2 pounds fresh mussels, cleaned and debearded
½ cup cream
Salt and freshly ground black pepper
1 cup loosely packed parsley leaves, roughly chopped
Crusty bread, for serving

1. Select a medium stockpot with a tight-fitting lid, and heat on medium. Once the pot is hot, lightly coat the surface with oil and add butter. When the butter begins to foam, add the garlic, and cook until just translucent.

2. Add the breadcrumbs to the pot and cook, stirring constantly, until crumbs are lightly brown. (Be careful—they burn easily.) Transfer breadcrumbs to a serving bowl.

3. Return the pot to the stove, add vegetable broth, and bring to a simmer. Add the mussels and half the bread crumb mixture, stir once, and cover. Cook 6 to 8 minutes, until the mussels have opened, discarding any that remain closed.

4. Use a slotted spoon to transfer the mussels to the serving bowl. Add the cream to the pot and cook for 2 to 3 minutes, scraping up the remaining breadcrumbs and garlic from the bottom, until cream is slightly thickened. Add salt and pepper to taste.
5. Pour the sauce over the mussels, top with remaining breadcrumbs and parsley, and serve immediately with warm crusty bread.

PETE'S MEAT PIES

Most folks who find themselves face-to-face with Colossus have trouble seeing anything beyond his massive metallic muscles. But my pal Piotr is more than just a paragon of platinum perfection. I love it when he decides to embrace his softer side, especially when he cooks up these traditional piroshki his mama used to make back on the Ust-Ordynsky Collective in Siberia. They're soft and delicate on the outside, with a powerful dose of meaty goodness in the middle . . . almost like a reverse Colossus!

—Deadpool

PETE'S MEAT PIES

Prep Time: 2 hours 15 minutes | **Cook Time:** 30 minutes
Yield: 24 piroshki

DOUGH:

1 package (2¼ teaspoons) active dry yeast
½ cup milk, room temperature
3 tablespoons unsalted butter, melted
1 egg, room temperature
½ tablespoon granulated sugar
½ teaspoon kosher salt
¼ teaspoon dried dill
2½ cups all-purpose flour

FILLING:

1 to 2 tablespoons olive oil, for pan
1 onion, finely chopped
1 shallot, finely chopped
1 pound ground beef
2 eggs, plus 1 for egg wash
3 tablespoons sour cream

1 tablespoon red wine vinegar
1 tablespoon Worcestershire sauce
2 tablespoons minced fresh dill (or 1 tablespoon dried)
2 teaspoons kosher salt
Freshly ground black pepper, to taste

SAUCE:
1 cup sour cream
2 tablespoons fresh dill (or 1 tablespoon dried)
1 tablespoon Worcestershire sauce
1 teaspoon kosher salt
1 teaspoon garlic powder
¼ teaspoon paprika

1. **TO MAKE THE DOUGH:** Dissolve the yeast in ¼ cup of water and let stand for 2 minutes. Combine the yeast mixture with the rest of the dough ingredients in the bowl of a stand mixer (or large bowl if mixing by hand), and mix with dough hook on low until a soft dough is formed. Turn the dough out onto a lightly floured surface, and knead until elastic, about 5 minutes. Place the dough in a lightly greased bowl, cover with a towel, and put in a warm place to rise for about 1½ hours or until doubled in size.

2. **WHILE THE DOUGH IS RISING, MAKE THE FILLING:** Coat a sauté pan with oil, and heat on medium. Add onion and shallot, and cook until just starting to brown, 5 to 7 minutes. Add the ground beef, and cook, stirring to break up the meat, until brown, about 5 minutes more. Move the mixture to one side of the pan and crack 2 eggs into the space. Let the eggs cook briefly before using your spatula to lightly break them up and mix them with the beef. Continue stirring until the egg is cooked through. Remove the pan from heat and add the remaining filling ingredients. Stir until well combined.

3. **TO ASSEMBLE:** Line 2 baking sheets with silicone mats or parchment paper. Using your hands and a scale, if you have one, form 24 equal dough balls, and place them on the baking sheets. Cover the sheets with a cloth while working. Use the palm of your hand to flatten each dough ball into a 3- to 3½-inch circle and fill with 2 mounded tablespoons of filling. Moisten the edge of each dough circle, fold over the filling, and pinch closed.

4. Place back on the baking sheet, seam-side down, and gently form into an oval rather than a half-moon. Repeat with remaining pies, covering each tray with a cloth when done. Let the pies rise until puffy, 30 to 40 minutes. Midway through the rise, preheat the oven to 350°F.

5. Beat the remaining egg with 1 tablespoon of water and brush each pie completely with egg wash. Bake until golden brown, about 20 minutes.

6. **TO MAKE THE SAUCE:** Mix all the ingredients together until well blended.

7. Serve the meat pies warm or at room temperature with sauce on the side.

FIND MORE RECIPES FROM

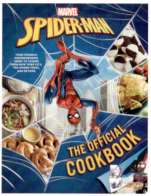

INSIGHT
EDITIONS

PO Box 3088
San Rafael, CA 94912
www.insighteditions.com

Find us on Facebook:
www.facebook.com/InsightEditions

Follow us on Instagram:
@insighteditions

© 2025 MARVEL

All rights reserved. This revised edition published by Insight Editions, San Rafael, California, in 2025.

No part of this book may be reproduced in any form without written permission from the publisher.

ISBN: 979-8-88663-899-8

Publisher: Raoul Goff
SVP, Group Publisher: Vanessa Lopez
VP, Creative: Chrissy Kwasnik
VP, Manufacturing: Alix Nicholaeff
Editorial Director: Thom O'Hearn
Art Director: Stuart Smith
Designer: Brooke McCullum
Associate Editor: Sami Alvarado
VP, Senior Executive Project Editor: Vicki Jaeger
Managing Editor: Shannon Ballesteros
Production Manager: Deena Hashem
Strategic Production Planner:
Lina s Palma-Temena

 REPLANTED PAPER

Insight Editions, in association with Roots of Peace, will plant two trees for each tree used in the manufacturing of this product.

Manufactured in China by Insight Editions

10 9 8 7 6 5 4 3 2 1

RECIPE SOURCES

Pages 9, 13, 17, 21, 25, 29, 35, 39, 45 .... previously published in *Marvel: Spider-Man: The Official Cookbook* by Paul Eschbach, Jermaine McLaughlin, and Von Diaz in 2024.

Pages 49, 53, 57, 61, 64, 66, 68, 71 .... previously published in *Marvel's Black Panther: The Official Wakanda Cookbook* by Nyanyika Banda and Jesse J. Holland in 2022.

Pages 75, 79, 83, 86, 89, 92, 96, 100, 105 .... previously published in *Marvel Comics: Cooking with Deadpool* by Elena P. Craig and Marc Sumerak in 2021.